# RELATIONSHIP RESILIENCE

# RELATIONSHIP RESILIENCE

## *Strengthening Bonds That Last*

AVERY NIGHTINGALE

Creative Quill Press

# CONTENTS

# CHAPTER 1

# Introduction

Permanently adjusting to the couple concept over a period is the best thing that can happen to the relationship. Be a good observer, show an empathetic attitude. You took her hand; you made the decision to take the half walking. Consider it with closeness. Practice active listening during your discussions: it is important that listening to the partner should be done in a supportive manner, leads the Italian website. The most useful thing you can do is cheer the person you're talking to. "As a result, you better resist all acts of total destruction. Resilient partners know to cheer each other and keep each other's spirits up. It is essential to be willing to administer more than one contact in the relationship fabric so as not to lose balance. When an act occurs that threatens the unit of the relationship, both partners must be able to readjust the clarity and well-being to find a new balance and the relationship should be improved," states the advice published on the website.

Strengthening the bonds of your relationship can be invaluable for many aspects of life, from your health and well-being to your overall happiness and ability to function well. Regularly practicing relationship resilience could lead to a lasting bond that can help you accompany and thrive together throughout life. What can you do every day to strengthen your bond? It's the small things each day that matter most. "Think of your partner as every individual who deserves to be listened to, asked about their experiences, not to be interrupted and not to be excluded," states the American psychological expert suggesting a basic principle of happiness in relationships.

# CHAPTER 2

# Understanding Relationship Resilience

All intimate relationships have likely found themselves in stressful situations. Many of these have navigated these difficult times successfully. Yet in a time in which many families find themselves in challenging financial circumstances, it is equally the case that there has been an increase in intimate partner violence. Many marriages stand the test of challenging times and remain happy and stable. Many marriages do not manage this difficult time in a way that serves to tear at the very fabric of the unit. What factors contribute to a relationship's avoidance of this risk? What contributes temporally? Is there anything that can be determined that relates to these factors prior to the risk/protective factor relationship that might help us to be proactive in ensuring that the risk does not overwhelm the protective? There are a number of different perspectives on the factors that may be associated with relationship resilience. A dynamic systems perspective might suggest that the interaction of partners leads to closeness and disconnection, or that the skills within a relationship (e.g. emotion regulation techniques) available to them. Others might suggest that resilience is innate, representing stable properties of relationships and individuals rather than arising from emerging processes within a relationship.

One trend in the study of intimate relationships involves the examination of factors that are associated with resilient rather than maladaptive associations. This shift in focus is important in that it helps us to identify the ways in which distress and deterioration can be avoided or mitigated, rather than simply noting vulnerability factors. Over 20 years ago, Block (1991) discussed the distinction between people whose lives were marked by various protective factors (i.e. the psychologically stable) and those in which damaging factors were prominent enough to suggest that they would lead to significant problems (i.e. the psychologically troubled). Relational resilience refers to the tendency for a relationship to avoid, or otherwise deal with, the risk factors that might typically threaten its stability.

## 2.1. Definition and Importance

It can be observed that those couples who are resilient manage to emerge strengthened from the confrontation against adversity, turning it into an element of strengthening and enhancing the relationship, not as occurs to other couples who are governed by non-stick routines that exacerbate insubstantial small problems, until becoming something insurmountable, that in the worst of cases forces them not to stay together. Nor should it be associated with feeling big for both members of the couple, and that therefore they are always going to be the exception of what does not suffer, as the majority of the others. Furthermore, those who are resilient will make it clear that it is very difficult to overcome all the samples of forces of the other enchantment, making their union solidifying when the ties with the partner are stimulated.

In present times, when the fastest, easiest goal is sought after and patience is not commonly trained, resilience is the key to counteract this issue, mainly realizing that we are forever living in a stable but at once unstable environment. In the case of relationships, resilience refers to the construction of strong and optimally functioning relationships through challenges. The commitment taken within couples decreases the chances of them being together in unhappy relationships, as well as between interdependent relationships. When discussing the particular case of intimate relationships, it is assumed that resilience arises from the positive elements of the relationship. Having friends with significant social support results in increased levels of resilience in the relationships. The promotion of activities in common that can be developed mutually, depending on the interaction of the pair, produces better solutions and feelings of well-being. It also helps to generate strength by increasing social capital, or the intangible resource related to the network of relationships where confidence, cooperation, and shared behaviors are shown.

### 2.2. Factors Affecting Relationship Resilience

There are many factors that may affect the level of resilience in individuals and in relationships. Starting with individuals, the effects of stress, according to person by stress interaction theory, are said to be the result of moderating variables which interact with each other. In the case of individuals, it has been suggested that optimists experience less damaging effects from stress than less optimistic individuals. If similar systems are in place for relationships, couples who are more optimistic may also do a better job of insulating their relationship from the ill effects of stress, ultimately reducing the risk of divorce. The relationship partner also affects the relationship. If both individuals are able to maintain their ability to be sensitive and responsive in the face of relationship stress, they may be better prepared to restore unity and harmony to the relationship when facing challenges. Resilient couples may also continuously search for supportive social ties when faced with challenges. Individuals without strong social ties often seek solace in blaming their partners for problems, which may lead to further bitterness, withdrawal, and distancing in connection. Social networks may serve as a buffer to relationship stress by teaching successful coping behaviors, sharing useful knowledge, and providing social support that encourages the couple to be hopeful about their ability to withstand tests and trials.

Relationship resilience describes the ability of couples to withstand and overcome the pressures that often lead to separation and divorce.

Collectively, studies in this course of research suggest that resilience in relationships, much like resilience in individuals, results from complex, emotionally charged interactions involving many checks and balances. Over time, partners develop internal working models that lead to couple interaction patterns, which then result in stress and physical health effects on both individuals. While the negative impact of stress on the relationship is clear, there is some evidence to suggest that either or both partners' level of resilience - defined as the ability to maintain one's sense of positivity and hope for the future in the face of negative life disruptions - can halt, or even reverse, the negative trajectory underlying individual and relationship well-being.

# CHAPTER 3

# Building Relationship Resilience

Doing fun things with your family helps grow happiness, excitement, and good feelings about one another. One of the neatest things about having fun with your partner and children is that you tend to smile and laugh lots. Smiling and laughing produce a chemical in your body that creates happiness and more good feelings for everyone. When this happens, it links everyone enjoying the same fun activity. These fun feelings form positive bonds with each other that build relationship resilience. Researchers found that families who took the time to strive to have fun together also yielded many good results. These families discovered that they had less stress within their own relationships and were able to find many positive experiences they all had participated in. Having fun with your children and your partner provides practical, 'real life' learning experiences that, in turn, helps grow relationship resilience. Bonds of resilience give families the extra safety they need in order to help lessen the impact of any negative interactions when an argument erupts.

You now know that resilience is being able to bounce back after experiencing difficulties, and that personal and family resilience is important in being able to maintain healthy and satisfying relationships. Building resilience can help your relationship strength remain strong. Families change many times as everyone grows in the relationship. These changes can produce some growing pains. Sometimes it's how families adapt together that can help the growing process become more comfortable for everyone. These experiences can also help you gain more confidence and strength as you face new experiences. Investing time, amendment, and energy into your relationship can make it more resilient. Resilient means it remains strong and can work even better after enduring some rough times.

### 3.1. Effective Communication

Effective communication in a relationship also involves the ability of the couple to disclose something personal to each other. For example, couples can openly discuss their behaviors, thoughts, and feelings. Disclosures of personal experiences are highly interconnected with the level of trust. When individuals reveal something deep to their partner, the emotional transparency helps to maintain the connection over time and can also predict the stability of the couple. Many people are uncomfortable disclosing things about their private lives. However, this is an essential strategy that can drive the couple to work together towards achieving common goals that are consistent with their relationship. In the case of low self-disclosure, couples may experience feelings of rejection as if they are not being told something.

Communication is an essential aspect of relationships. No relationship is immune to problems, and without the ability to talk through the inevitable minor issues that arise daily, these small problems can lead to greater misunderstanding and discontent. Open and effective communication can help couples maintain a sense of openness and interdependence. This enables them to approach everything as a joint effort. Couples should learn to express their thoughts and emotions about what affects them to their loved ones. This is of significant importance because when discussing significant matters, the couple communicates emotional support. Expressing emotions and affirmations is the foundation of emotional responsiveness and conveys the message that one person is open, interested, and available despite busy work schedules.

### 3.2. Trust and Forgiveness

In particular, forgiveness has been found an essential element of trusting relationships. The ability to forgive is the ability to replace chaotic thoughts and feelings with decision-making, empathy, and compassion. Studies show that forgiving others helps people to repair problematic relationships, to have social support, and to avoid excess competition. Accordingly, studies have suggested that people who have the opportunity to express forgiveness report intense feelings toward their partner, their relationship, fairer treatment towards their partner, a more optimistic vision of the future with their partner, and are more likely to remember the positive things in their relationships. It is important to remember that forgiveness should not be confused with legitimization, condoning, reconciliation, absolution, or forgetting. As Spahel explains, "If you think you've forgiven someone, but you still talk about it and nurse your grievances, that's resentment. Shouldering resentment while at the same time faking forgiveness can unnerve us with self-righteousness, the network of which can act on the brain because it isn't a very comfortable or satisfying mood.

Trust and forgiveness. A common feature of all resilient relationships is the presence of trust. Trust is the firm belief in the reliability, truth, or ability of someone. It is the confidence in the power of something. It requires courage and commitment, as various relationship studies reveal. Trust is the critical foundation for all intrapersonal and interpersonal relationships. According to them, without trust, positive relationships are not possible, and "without trust, the ability to create strong relationships is over." One significant component of trust is faith in the other's goodwill, regardless of their behavior or character. Trust concerns more certainty and motivation; it is the belief that the other intends to act in a positive, desired, agreed manner, and it raises the person's positive emotions.

### 3.3. Managing Conflict

Having a joint goal in mind can reduce strong emotions during a fight. After a dispute, especially one that is not solved, some partners will feel hurt, angry, suspicious, or emotionally bruised. It will be important to hold talks about ongoing struggles and decide how to resolve the problem together to ensure a long-lasting, strong, stable, and happy marriage. Avoid blaming and opt for words that allow joint problem-solving. This can draw on a wealth of patience, resilience, and mutual concern for personal growth. Being reminded that a partner is a human person who is vulnerable to injury, offense, and psychological pain will help control a volatile situation. Research has shown that it is a solid relationship in which both parties trust the depth of the love. A great way to train is by demonstrating the desire to learn about a personal matter carefully and respectfully. Another technique is to be sure to show enthusiastic conduct upon receipt of advice when tensions subside. Knowing that each spouse contributes can be both soothing and satisfying to each spouse when you work through a struggle.

An essential part of maintaining a relationship is handling conflict graciously. Disagreements are not often fun, but they can add depth and meaning to the relationship as each partner learns more about both the other and themselves. All of us are experienced in conflict either passively or actively. While it's unsettling and the idea of cheating is quite tempting, it is important to learn to settle a problem with respect and understanding. Learning how to avoid certain things when having strong, polarized opinions will also help to ensure that the partner who objects can still recognize it as an invitation to discuss an issue. The problem is examined by both partners and also contributes to their ongoing conflict.

### 3.4. Cultivating Emotional Connection

To be able to discuss these daily struggles and annoyances, it is necessary to not only have spent ample time getting to know one another, their personality idiosyncrasies, how they process emotions and thoughts, but also to be highly satisfied in their relationships. This ability to take action when angry to solve the daily desires, while still maintaining a connection in the relationship, is not only beneficial for relationship health but can also be useful in conflict resolution. More generally, accommodation is described as the balancing of individual and goals, with the consideration of what the partner values. It does not manifest as the avoidance or denial of needy discussion, a weakening of equanimity and feelings, negative affect and depressive cognitions. Such avoidant approaches to communication can express themselves via a lowering of conversational tools that are uniquely beneficial in re-establishing a healthy functioning relationship. Providing effective opportunities to disclose emotional experiences is pivotal to restoring emotional and practical attunement and the expression and occurrence; reliving these injuries promotes moving forward and treating the relationship with the intent to express emotional intimacy and experience connection.

We humans struggle mightily with expressing tender feelings and information with those we care about the most. We assume that report talk and independent functioning or privacy are paramount. In reality, it is vulnerability that most endears us to a partner. "This means that, to be fully effective in helping our husbands work with their emotions, we need to be genuinely interested in those emotions... This is quite different from keeping the lid on their emotions so they won't drive us mad." Emotion is vital to relationships and is evidenced in empathy and concerns about partner well-being. In one experiment, those who remained connected were partners who displayed empathy for their partners. These individuals exhibited good listener body language, vocalizations, liked and remarked on partner's words, and expressed concern and empathy without judgment. Even in cases of serious mammary cancer concerns, being open, honest, and displaying genuine care for a partner's well-being would help them to feel connected rather than protective. While the first recovery can be rated "normal" or hyperprotective, the strategy of expressing self-consciousness, feeling connected/ liked by the partner are rated as the secures at both ten and eighteen months post-surgery.

# CHAPTER 4

# Sustaining Relationship Resilience

We emphasize that if mutual consent or decision-making steers towards ending a relationship, exiting the relationship should be respectful without triggering punitive or painful outcomes, to either partner or others impacted by that bond. In relationships, capacity and agency towards decisional balance demonstrate its relationship resilience; reformation, a new component of mutual resilience, paves another path. In essence, relationship resilience is a broader and multi-faceted connective tissue precisely because of capacity, consent, and autonomy in decision making, and more so, as couples potentially safeguard and implement RQ in their unique ways.

The fourth sign of RQ, Sustaining Relationship Resilience (SRR RQ), becomes relevant in times when love and desire wane, when affection and goodwill towards your partner diminish, or when thoughts linger on a path that is easier than ushering in transformative change that relationship resilience may imply. The consensus in popular culture is that in relationships, passion fades, the spark fizzles out, and while these are predictable and impermanent, staying in a relationship indefinitely is rare. SRR RQ examines the types of systems and practices that support long-term sustainability in romantic relationships; specifically, the engine of routines and habits, the fuel of processes, and the force fields of elements that hold the couple together. SRR RQ draws parallels from sustainable architecture, sustainable supply chain, and community partnerships.

### 4.1. Nurturing Intimacy

Work on enhancing physical closeness. Studies show that when it comes to intimacy, physical closeness—being comfortable with hugs, cuddles, and caresses—is even more important than sex. In a secure relationship, basic tumbling and rolling around—the kind of wrestling that kids do without instruction—can create moments of trust and joy. Keep in mind that your relationship predicts future physical closeness, which is what women say they desire most in the early stages of their relationship. After about 15-20 minutes of teasing and rolling and some giggling, it's not uncommon for wrestling couples to engage in spontaneous kissing and caressing while rolling around on the floor. If you succeed in this wrestling fun time, you won't have to push too hard to make your partner feel warm, fuzzy, and loved. You can have "foreplay" without ever talking about sex or thinking about sex, and that leads to more and better-connected emotional and physical intimacy. Make wrestling a priority at least once a week. The more tumbling you do, the more playful and alive you'll feel—and that bond will deepen and grow in strength and resilience.

Intimacy between partners refers to the mutual depth of caring and loving feelings. When both partners openly share such emotions, disagreements decrease and commitment deepens. To nurture intimacy, make a list of what you like about yourself, then share this list with your partner. As you openly share such things, you help your partner feel closer and bond together. Minimize negativity and criticism, as well as crying. For deeper intimacy, you can pray or meditate together.

### 4.2. Balancing Individuality and Togetherness

When you have separate interests, and your lives are not completely intertwined, you can each explore your interests more fully and then come together to share and discuss. When you come together after some time apart, you'll also have new things to share with each other, even if you are doing the same activity you often do. One of the best things about spending time apart is the buildup of anticipation to see each other again. Let's think about a time when we've been away from our partner for a few hours. By the end of that time, we are probably counting the minutes until we can see them again!

You and your partner don't have to agree on everything or have the same interests to have a happy relationship. In fact, having differing opinions and pursuits can lead to robust rapport. The key is finding a balance between individuality and togetherness that works for you and your partner. You and your partner are entirely separate human beings with your own thoughts, feelings, beliefs, likes, dislikes, and characteristics. If we're to believe the old adage that opposites attract, then finding someone who sees and experiences the world in a way that is completely different from how you see and experience the world should not be considered a barrier, but rather an opportunity. While being with someone who is completely different from you may be challenging at times (potentially leading to a few good battles in the future), it can also be exhilarating. Your partner can offer you a new perspective, open you up to different experiences, and push you to see things in a new light.

### 4.3. Supportive Relationships Outside the Partnership

Greater feelings of love and marital happiness are reported in couples consisting of those with larger and diversified social networks. Indeed, when the extended family is still a vital part of relational life, the existing literature has long suggested that an intimate but diversified social network is beneficial for couples (e.g., physiological health outcomes, depression levels). In fact, the more in common couples have with social network members, the more supported couples feel. Sharing interests, goals, and relationships supports the concept that coupled faith, friendship, and kinship can mutually constitute positive social capital, resulting in highly satisfactory relationships. Finally, and in extreme situations, the value of keeping in touch as a couple also enhances relationship quality as gestalt can be maintained during relocation.

The codependency literature has provided the backdrop for understanding supportive relationships outside the partnership. Recent literature focusing on marriage has shown that partners connected to important others in addition to each other enhance relationship satisfaction, providing emotional support and encouragement that eases the stresses of everyday life. The off-loading phenomenon, for example, whereby a long-term partner comes to play many substantial roles that may otherwise be played by multiple others such as children, friends, and family, should be discouraged as sharing is an investment in marital happiness. Couples appear to be happier and stay together for longer when the partners are connected to important others other than themselves.

* 9 7 9 8 8 6 9 3 7 6 3 6 7 *